Prayers for Your New Baby

Chosen and illustrated
by Chris Coe

kevin
mayhew

A new baby – how wonderful! Children are God's priceless gift for the world to cherish, an expression of his loving-kindness.

As you read these carefully chosen prayers, poems and Bible verses, reflect on the miracle of new birth, knowing that your child is so precious to God and richly blessed by him.

Our heavenly Father will teach you love, patience and wisdom to nurture the new life entrusted to you. By his good grace your child will grow up strong in faith, learn to trust God and walk close to him.

Lord God, we thank you
for the great gift you give
the world, in children.
Give us grace to dedicate ourselves
to one another and to you,
to be channels to each other
of your priceless love,
freely given and
freely received.

Praise the Lord for he is good

Psalm 135:3

Children are a gift from the Lord

Psalm 127:3

God bless this baby,
newly born, with all the
gentle love of heaven.
A miracle, wrapped up
and fast asleep,
reminding us again
of human hope
and innocence.

Susan Sayers

Hush-a-bye baby,
here in your bed,
stars of the heavens shine
bright overhead.
Under your feet
is the planet of earth;
out of the universe
God gave you birth.

Susan Sayers

He will love you and bless you

Deuteronomy 7:13

Jesus took the children in his arms
and blessed them

Mark 10:16

Heavenly Father, give this child
a deep love of learning,
and the wisdom to understand
how to use the knowledge s/he gains.
May s/he know the joy of curiosity
and wonder in your beautiful world.
May s/he never stop asking questions.

Lord of all, bless this child
with a deep sense of joy and happiness
throughout their life.
When times are hard –
as sometimes they will be –
may s/he still have a thankful heart
for blessings received,
and for your faithful presence.

Susan Hardwick

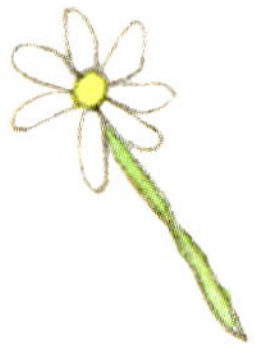

The Lord bless you
and keep you.
The Lord smile upon you,
and be kind to you.
The Lord look
with favour upon you,
and give you peace.

Numbers 6:24-26

Sing to the Lord all the earth

Psalm 96:1

The Lord blesses his people with peace

Psalm 29:11

Lord Jesus Christ, our Lord most dear,
as you were once an infant here,
so give this child of yours, we pray,
your grace and blessing day by day.

Their watch let angels round her/him keep
where'er s/he be, awake, asleep.
Be pleased your caring love to give,
and keep this child by morn and eve.

Heinrich von Laufenberg (15th Century)
trans. Catherine Winkworth (1827-78)

It fell upon a summer day,
when Jesus walked in Galilee,
the mothers from the village brought
their children to his knee.

He took them in his arms, and laid
his hands on each remembered head.
'Suffer these little ones to come
to me,' he gently said.

'Forbid them not. Unless you bear
the childlike heart your hearts within,
unto my kingdom you may come,
but may not enter in.'

Then, Jesus, look upon this child
that he may come to you and feel
your hands on him in blessing laid,
love-giving, strong to heal.

Stopford Augustus Brooke (1832-1916)

The Lord takes care of his people like a shepherd

Isaiah 40:11

This is the day that the Lord has made;
let us rejoice and be glad

Psalm 118:24

Heavenly Father,
we thank you from our hearts
for our new baby
whom you have sent into our lives
and put into our care.
We ask for grace and wisdom
as we take on the responsibility
for this new life.
May our child grow
in strength and health,
in knowledge and understanding,
and learn the joy
of walking in your ways,
through Jesus Christ our Lord.
Amen.

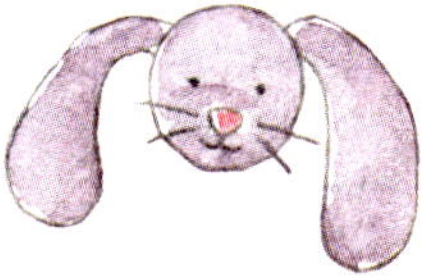

May you grow in strength, little one,
and use your strength for good.
May you grow in knowledge, little one,
and temper it with wisdom.
May you grow in faith, little one,
and learn to trust in God.
May you grow in love, little one,
and walk in it all your days.

Peter Dainty

Give thanks to the Lord!

Psalm 105:1

He has given us great and precious promises

2 Peter 1:4

Twinkle, twinkle little star,
how I wonder what you are.
God made you
and God made me,
made the moon
and sky and sea.
Twinkle, twinkle little star,
how I wonder what you are.

Susan Sayers

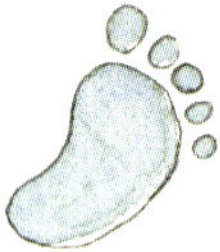

Precious one,
so small,
so sweet;

dancing in
on angel feet;
straight from
heaven's brightest star;

what a miracle
you are.

Lord you have done such great things

Psalm 92:5

Whoever welcomes one of these
little children in my name welcomes me

Mark 9:37

Every good and perfect gift
is from above,
coming down from the
Father of heavenly lights,
who does not change like
shifting shadows.

James 1:17

Almighty God
and heavenly Father,
we thank you for the children
which you have given to us.
Give us grace to bring them up
in your faith, reverence and love,
that as they advance in years,
they may grow in grace,
and be found in the number
of your own family;
through Jesus Christ our Lord.

John Cosin (1596-1672)

The Lord is good. His love continues for ever

Psalm 100:5

May the whole earth be filled with his glory

Psalm 72:19

And there were shepherds
living out in the fields near by,
keeping watch over their flocks at night.
An angel of the Lord appeared to them,
and the glory of the Lord
shone around them,
and they were terrified.
But the angel said to them,
'Do not be afraid. I bring you good news
of great joy that will be for all the people.
Today in the town of David
a Saviour has been born to you;
he is Christ the Lord.
This will be a sign to you:
you will find a baby wrapped in cloths
and lying in a manger.'

Luke 2:8-12

KEVIN MAYHEW LTD
Buxhall, Stowmarket, Suffolk, IP14 3BW
E-mail: info@kevinmayhewltd.com
Website: www.kevinmayhew.com

9 8 7 6 5 4 3 2 1 0

ISBN 978 1 84867 525 4
Catalogue No. 1501357

Design and illustrations by Chris Coe

Printed and bound in China